Late Intermediate Piano Duet

Concertino No. 2

Solo Piano, Two Pianos, or Solo Piano with Orchestra

By Anna Asch

Hal•Leonard®
CORPORATION

7777 W. BLUEMOUND RD. P.O. BOX 13819 MILWAUKEE, WI 53213

CONCERTINO NO. 2

(For Tara)

By ANNA ASCH

*Note: If playing as a solo, fill in from 2nd piano part as needed.

Written by Anna Asch

accel.

accel. e cresc.

More lively (♩ = 138)

f steady

More lively (♩ = 138)

f steady

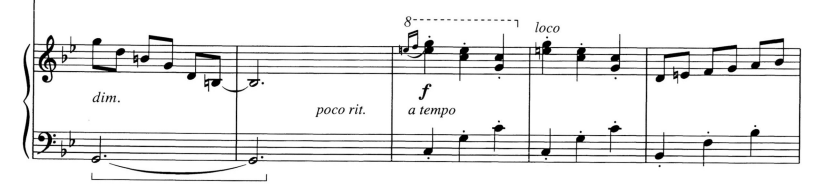

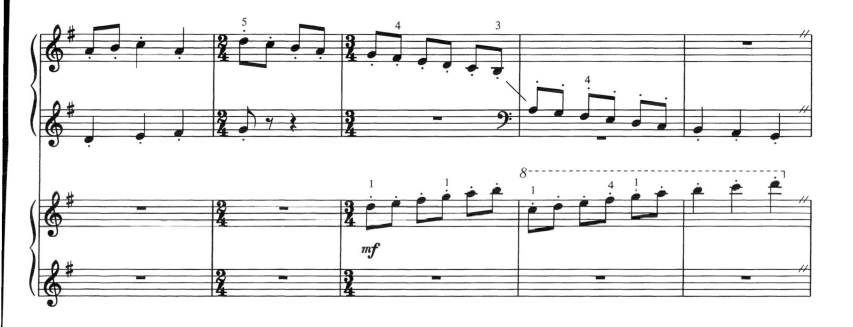

Orchestral score and parts available from:
AJA Arts, 7483 Brookhaven Road, West Bend, WI

ISBN-13: 978-0-7935-3759-4

Distributed By
HAL LEONARD

U.S. $7.99

HL00290473

00290473